KU-826-987

The Little Book of
Essential
Foreign Insults

Emma Burgess

summersdale

Summersdale Publishers Ltd
46 West Street
Chichester
PO19 1RP   UK

www.summersdale.com

ISBN 1 84024 385 6

Printed and bound in the EU.

With thanks to Pascal Guerin, Roberto Jimeno Barbara Schindler and Prof. Van Der Beak.

Contents

Introduction

Welcome, bienvenue, wilkommen, and various other insincere foreign platitudes to The Little Book of Essential Foreign Insults!

We all love a holiday – the sun, the sand, the sea, and the opportunity to tell a Johnny Foreigner where to stick his metaphorical, er, stick. In my first œuvre, *The Little Book of Essential Foreign Swear Words* (TLBOEFSW*), I gave you the building blocks to swear your *pelotas* off at the natives of your most likely holiday destination. With this lifesaver of a book I present you with the metaphorical mortar and trowel with which to build a nice wall between you and the stinky locals. But be sure to invest in a hard hat.

And don't forget, when people tell you that it's not big or clever, just tell them that it's 9 inches long and has a degree in History.

Irreverently yours,

The Ambassador of Insults

---

*A useful acronym for you – an anagram of which is BESTFLOW, by the way. OK, I know that's completely pointless, but then so are foreign types, aren't they?

THE LITTLE BOOK OF

Fuck off!

French:
Va te faire foutre!

German:
Verpiß Dich!

Italian:
Vaffanculo!

Spanish:
Vete a tomar por culo!

THE LITTLE BOOK OF

You cunt!

French:
Con!

German:
Fotze!

Italian:
Fica!

Spanish:
Cono!

Wanker!

"

French:
Branleur!

German:
Wichser!

Italian:
Mezza sega!

Spanish:
Gilipollas!

Kiss my arse!

French:
Touche ton cul!

German:
Läck mich am Arsch!

Italian:
Leccami il culo!

Spanish:
Puedes besar mi culo!

Get out of my sight!

French:
Dégage de ma vue!

German:
Mach das du weg kommst!

Italian:
Sparisci!

Spanish:
Fuera de mi vista!

GENERIC

I hope you die!

French:
Vas crever!

German:
Erlöse uns und Stirb schon!

Italian:
Crepa!

Spanish:
Espero que te mueras!

GENERIC

I hate you!

French:
Je te déteste!

German:
Ich haße dich!

Italian:
Ti odio!

Spanish:
Te odio!

A pox on your throat!

French:
Véreux!

German:
Eine Wartze am Nacken!

Italian:
Ti colga la peste!

Spanish:
Como un pincho en tu garganta!

GENERIC

You fat bastard!

French:
Gros bâtard!

German:
Du fette Sau!

Italian:
Grasso bastardo!

Spanish:
Gordo cabron!

Shove it up your arse!

French:
Enfonce-le-toi dans le cul!

German:
Steckst dir im Hintern!

Italian:
Mettitelo nel culo!

Spanish:
Saca eso de tu trasero!

GENERIC

Get lost!

French:
Va mourir!

German:
Hau ab!

Italian:
Sparisci!

Spanish:
Pierdete!

Go fuck yourself!

French:
Va te la mettre!

German:
Verpiß dich schon!

Italian:
Fatti una sega!

Spanish:
Vete a follar!

Ugly fucker!

French:
Sale enculé!

German:
Häßliches Arschloch!

Italian:
Brutto stronzo!

Spanish:
Guarro!

You pointless twat!

French:
Pauvre crétin!

German:
Du unnoteiges unwesen!

Italian:
Inetto imbecille!

Spanish:
Eres muy puta!

Cocksucker!

French:
Lécheur de boule !

German:
Schwanzlecker!

Italian:
Ciucciacazzo!

Spanish:
Chupa pollas!

" How fascinating, I've never seen a country with so many peasants. Oh sorry, I didn't realise they're your royal family. "

French:

C'est fascinant, je n'ai jamais vu un pays avec autant de paysans. Oh, désolé! Je n'ai pas réalisé que c'était votre famille royale!

German:

Faszinierend, Ich habe nie ein Land mit so viel Proletariat gesehen. Verzeihen Sie, Ich habe nicht erkannt daß sie Ihre Königlich Familie waren.

Italian:

Interessante. Non ho mai visto un paese con così tanti contadini. O scusi, non sapevo che si trattasse della famiglia reale.

Spanish:

Que fascinante! Nunca antes vi un país con tantos palurdos. Perdón! No sabía que fueran la Familia Real.

100% XENOPHOBIC

Is 'Johnny Foreigner' your real name?

French:
'Métèque', c'est
vraiment votre nom?

German:
Ist Johhny der Fremde
dein echter Name?

Italian:
Bingo Bongo è il
tuo vero nome?

Spanish:
Es 'Johnny el extranjero'
tu verdadero nombre?

100% XENOPHOBIC

If this country were my home, I would seek asylum elsewhere faster than you can say 'fake ID'.

French:

Si ce pays était le mien, je demanderai l'asile partout ailleurs avant même que vous ayez pu prononcer «faux-papiers».

German:

Wenn dieses Land mein zu Hause wäre, wûrde ich schneller anderswo Asyl beantragen als Du einen Ausweis verfälschen könntest.

Italian:

Se questo paese fosse il mio cercherei asilo altrove prima che tu abbia il tempo di dire "documenti falsi".

Spanish:

Si este pais fuera mi casa, buscaria asilo en otro lugar antes que puedas decir 'documeto de identidad falso'.

100% XENOPHOBIC

If you could just listen to yourself ... that accent of yours is ridiculous.

French:
Si seulement vous vous écoutiez …
Votre accent est tellement ridicule.

German:
Hör dich doch an …
dein akzent ist lächerlich.

Italian:
Se tu ti potessi sentire…
Il tuo accento è veramente ridicolo.

Spanish:
Si te escucharas … encontrarias
ridiculo tu acento.

100% XENOPHOBIC

The only decent thing we have between us would be ... the sea.

French:
La seule chose d'honorable qu'il y aurait
entre nous, ce serait ... La mer.

German:
Das einzig gute zwischen uns wäre
etwa ... der Englische Kanal.

Italian:
L'unica cosa che dovremmo
avere fra noi è ... il mare.

Spanish:
Lo unico decente que
compartimos es ... el mar.

100% XENOPHOBIC

It's a bit selfish of you not to speak English, don't you think?

French:
C'est un peu égoïste de votre part de ne pas parler anglais, vous ne trouvez pas?

German:
Es ist ziemlich unverschämt daß Sie nicht Englisch sprechen, meinen Sie nicht?

Italian:
Non (saper) parlare inglese è un po' egoista da parte tua, non credi?

Spanish:
Es egoista por tu parte no hablar ingles. No lo crees asi?

100% XENOPHOBIC

Do you serve drinks with ice that isn't made from faecal deposits?

French:
Servez-vous des glaçons qui ne contiennent pas de matière fécale?

German:
Servieren Sie Getränke mit Eis daß nicht von hintelaßene Scheiße gemacht worden ist?

Italian:
Mettete mai nelle bibite del ghiaccio che non sia merda?

Spanish:
El hielo de las bebidas procede de depositos fecales?

FOOD / DRINK

Your beer tastes like old man's wee.

French:
Votre bière a le goût du pipi de vieux.

German:
Ihr Bier schmeckt nach kränkliche Altersheimpiße.

Italian:
La vostra birra sa di piscia di gatto.

Spanish:
Tu cerveza sabe a orina de viejo.

Do you have anything edible on your menu?

French:
Auriez-vous quelque chose de comestible sur votre menu?

German:
Gibts etwas esbares auf Ihrem Menu?

Italian:
Avete niente di commestibile sul menu?

Spanish:
Tiene algo comestible en el menu?

Where I come from, we walk the family pet ... not eat it.

French:
Chez moi, les animaux de compagnie on les promène, on ne les bouffe pas.

German:
Bei uns zu Lande nehmen wir unsere Haustiere mit spazieren … nicht als Vorspeise.

Italian:
Nel mio paese gli animali domestici li portiamo a spasso, non li mangiamo.

Spanish:
De donde yo vengo, paseamos a las mascotas … no nos las comemos.

FOOD / DRINK

Thanks to your disgusting local cuisine, dieting has never been so easy.

French:
Merci pour la cuisine locale
dégueulasse, faire un régime n'a
jamais été aussi facile.

German:
Dank Ihrer scheuslischen
einheimische Küche, fiel mir das
Abnehmen nie so leicht.

Italian:
Con la vostra cucina schifosa non
è mai stato così facile stare a dieta.

Spanish:
Gracias por tu desagradable cocina,
nunca fue tan facil ponerse a dieta.

FOOD / DRINK

I have a little irritation down below. Ah yes, I see it's Europe. In that case, there's no cure.

French:

J'ai une légère démangeaison mal placée. Ah ! Je vois, c'est l'Europe. Dans ce cas, il n'y a aucun remède.

German:

Mir juckts recht schlecht am Arsch. Ach ja, das wäre etwa Europa. Deshalb gibt's auch kein Heilmittel.

Italian:

Ho del prurito laggiù. Ah, è l'Europa. Beh, in questo caso non c'è rimedio.

Spanish:

Tengo algo irritate ahy abajo. Oh! Ya veo. Es Europa. En ese caso, no tiene solucion.

Do you have a hose-pipe I could borrow? Your country needs colonic irrigation.

French:
Pourrai-je vous emprunter un tuyau d'arrosage? Votre pays a besoin d'un lavement.

German:
Kanst Du mir mal 'nen Schlauch leihen? Dein Land hat 'ne Arschdurchspülung nötig.

Italian:
Hai un tubo da prestare?
Il vostro paese ha bisogno
di un'irrigazione anale.

Spanish:
Tienes alguna manguera que pueda tomar prestada? Tu pais necesita ser regado por colonialistas.

HEALTH & SAFETY

So that's what syphilis looks like. Are there any other indigenous conditions that I should know about?

French:
Voila donc a quoi ressemble la Syphilis.
Y a t-il d'autres affections typiques que je
devrais connaître?

German:
So sieht Syfilis aus. Gibt's weitere
einheimische Erkrankungen über die ich
mich informieren sollte?

Italian:
Quindi questa è la sifilide…
Ci sono altre malattie locali di cui
dovrei essere al corrente?

Spanish:
Asi que eso es la siphilis. Hay alguna otra
enfermedad que debo conocer?

HEALTH & SAFETY

Is it normal to foam at the mouth like that?

French:
Est-ce normal cette écume au bord de la bouche comme cela?

German :
Ist das normal so am Mund zu schaumen?

Italian:
È normale avere la bava alla bocca così?

Spanish:
Es normal echar espuma por la boca de eso manera?

I spent a week in the departure lounge before I finally got to your country. It was the best week of the holiday.

French:
J'ai passé une semaine dans un salon d'embarquement avant d'arriver enfin dans votre pays. C'était la plus belle semaine de toutes mes vacances.

German:
Ich habe 'ne ganze Woche im Wartesaal beim Abflug verbracht. Das war die beste Woche meines Urlaubs.

Italian:
Ho passato una settimana nella sala partenze prima di arrivare finalmente nel vostro paese. E' stata la migliore settimana della vacanza.

Spanish:
Espere una semana en la sala de embarque antes de llegar a tu pais. Fue lo mejor de las vacaciones.

HOLIDAY / TRANSPORT

Our trains back home smell nearly as bad as yours.

French:
Les trains chez nous sentaient presque
aussi mauvais que les vôtres.

German:
Unsere Bahnzüge stinken fast so
schlecht wie Eure.

Italian:
I nostri treni puzzano
quasi come i vostri.

Spanish:
Nuestro tren de regreso a casa olia
tan mal como el tuyo.

This is a one-way street and so is my arse, for the record.

French:
C'est une rue à sens unique,
comme mon cul, pour votre gouverne.

German:
Dies ist 'ne Einbahnstraße – und ebenso
mein Arsch – nur daß Du es weist!

Italian:
Questa è una strada a senso unico,
come il mio culo, per tua informazione.

Spanish:
Esta calle es de unico sentido y no es por
detras. Para vuestra informacion.

HOLIDAY / TRANSPORT

You stink of shit.

French:
Vous puez la merde.

German:
Du stinkst nach Scheiße.

Italian:
Puzzi di merda.

Spanish:
Apestas a mierda.

SMELLS / DIRT

Is that rotting flesh or your armpits that I can smell?

French:
Est-ce de la viande avariée ou vos aisselles cette odeur?

German:
Ist das verfaulte Haut oder deine Unterarme die ich da rieche?

Italian:
E' odore di carne andata a male o sono le tue ascelle?

Spanish:
Huele a carne podrida o son tus sobacos?

It smells like I've got some shit stuck to my shoe – yes, it's your country.

French:
Ca sent comme si j'avais de la merde collée sous la chaussure – bien oui, c'est votre pays.

German:
Es stinkt so als ob ich Hundescheiße auf die Schuhe habe – ach ja, es hängt von Ihrem Land ab.

Italian:
Puzza come se avessi della merda attaccata alla scarpa – ah, è il vostro paese.

Spanish:
Huele como si llevara algo de mierda en mi zapato. Ya veo, es tu pais.

SMELLS / DIRT

77

Why has no one thought of importing deodorants to your country?

French:
Pourquoi personne n'a jamais pensé a importer du déodorant dans votre pays?

German:
Wieso hat man noch nie Deo Sprüh in Ihrem Land eingeführt?

Italian:
Perché nessuno ha mai pensato di importare deodoranti nel vostro paese?

Spanish:
Por que no se piensa en importar desodorantes a tu pais?

We must be near the sea, I can smell fish. Whoops, it's your red light district.

French:
On ne doit pas être très loin de la mer,
ça sent le poisson. Oh! Pardon, on
est dans le quartier des bordels.

German:
Sind wir etwa an der Küste, es
riecht nach Fisch. Ach so, hier
gibt's lauter Bordellen.

Italian:
Dobbiamo essere vicini al mare,
sento odore di pesce. Oh, è
il vostro quartiere a luci rosse…

Spanish:
Debemos estar cerca del mar. Puedo
oler a pescado. Oh! Es el
distrito de las putas.

Your coastline could do with a clean up ... a tsunami might do the trick.

French:
Votre littoral aurait besoin d'un coup de propre. Un raz-de-marée ferait l'affaire.

German:
Ihre Küste ist ziemlich verschmutzt.
Ein Tsunami könnte schon
als Reinigung reichen.

Italian:
La vostra costa ha bisogno di una pulita…
uno tsunami potrebbe andar bene.

Spanish:
Vendria bien limpiar el litoral … un
tsunami podria hacerlo.

SMELLS / DIRT

83

**I'd like to meet
your parents.
When is the
zoo open?**

French:
J'aimerai bien rencontrer vos parents?
Vous connaissez les horaires
d'ouverture du zoo?

German:
Ich würde schon gerne deine Eltern
treffen. Wan hat der Zoo offen?

Italian:
Vorrei conoscere i tuoi genitori.
Quando apre lo zoo?

Spanish:
Me gustaria conocer a tus padres.
Cuando esta el zoo abierto?

IN-BREEDING

Are you sick? I'll call the emergency vet.

French:
Vous êtes malade? Je vais appeler
un vétérinaire en urgence.

German:
Bist du Krank? Ich ruf schon
mal den Tierartzt.

Italian:
Ti senti male? Chiamo
l'emergenza veterinaria.

Spanish:
Estas enfermo?
Llamare al veterinario.

IN-BREEDING

Nice hair. Does it grow all over your back?

French:
Belle toison! Vous en avez le long
du dos également?

German:
Schone Haare hast du. Wachsen
sie am ganzen Rücken?

Italian:
Che bei capelli.
Ti crescono su tutta la schiena?

Spanish:
Bonito pelo. Lo tienes igual
por todo el cuerpo?

IN-BREEDING

THE LITTLE BOOK OF

I guess shagging your siblings conveniently precludes the need for dating agencies.

French:
Je suppose que de baiser entre frères et sœurs vous épargne les services d'une agence matrimoniale.

German:
Ich vermute daß vor lauter sex innerhalb der Verwandschaft, sie Partner Treff oder Dating nicht nötig haben.

Italian:
Penso che far sesso con i tuoi parenti ti eviti la necessità di contattare agenzie matrimoniali.

Spanish:
Follar con tus hermanos hace innecesarias las agencias matrimoniales.

IN-BREEDING

In my country it's not normal for women to have hair there.

French:
Dans mon pays, il est normal pour les femmes d'avoir des poils à cet endroit.

German:
In unserem Land haben Fraün in dem Bereich normalerweise keine Haare.

Italian:
Nel mio paese non è normale che le donne abbiano peli là.

Spanish:
En mi pais, las mujeres no suelen tener pelo en el cono.

SEXUAL

93

Ropy old whore!

French:
Vieille pute visqueuse!

German:
Verseuchte alte Nutte.

Italian:
Vecchia bagascia schifosa!

Spanish:
Vieja puta!

Thanks to you, it now hurts when I wee.

French:
Merci à vous, maintenant ça me
brûle quand je pisse.

German:
Du bist zu danken dafür das es
beim pißen weh tut.

Italian:
Grazie a te, ora mi fa
male quando faccio piscio.

Spanish:
Gracias a ti, ahora me duele
cuando meo.

SEXUAL

Where I come from, foreplay doesn't mean 'one up the arse'.

French:
Chez moi, préliminaire ne signifie
pas «se faire limer avant».

German:
Wo ich herstamme ist Arschficken
nicht gelich eine Form von Anmachung.

Italian:
Da dove vengo io, preliminari
non vuol dire "inculare".

Spanish:
De donde yo vengo, terminar de
follar no significa tener que
dar por culo.

THE LITTLE BOOK OF

I seem to have completely lost my sex drive since visiting your country.

French:
Je semble avoir perdu tout appétit
sexuel depuis que j'ai visité votre pays.

German:
Seit dem ich bei Dir im Land bin bin
ich nicht mehr an Sex interesert.

Italian:
Da quando mi trovo nel vostro paese mi
sembra di aver completamente perso la
voglia di fare sesso.

Spanish:
He perdido completamente mi deseo de
follar desde que visite tu pais.

SEXUAL

You have a great face ... for radio.

French:
Vous avez un visage magnifique …
pour faire de la radio.

German:
Du hast ein tolles Gesicht …
für Radio.

Italian:
Hai la faccia perfetta…
per la radio.

Spanish:
Tienes una bonita cara …
para la radio.

UGLY

103

I don't know how to describe you. Is there a stronger word than ugly?

French:
Je ne sais pas comment vous décrire.
Y a t-il un mot plus fort que moche?

German:
Ich weiß nicht wie ich Dich am besten
beschreiben sollte. Gibt's da was
stärkeres als häßlich?

Italian:
Non so descriverti.
Esiste una parola più forte di mostruoso?

Spanish:
No sabria como describirte. Hay
alguna palabra mas fuerte que feo?

UGLY

I may be drunk, but in the morning I'll be sober and you'll still be ugly.

French:
J'ai peut-être bu, mais demain matin
je serai sobre et vous serez
oujours aussi moche.

German:
Heut' Abend bin ich vielleicht besoffen
aber morgen Früh bist du noch häßlich.

Italian:
Lo sarò anche ubriaco, ma domani mattina
io sarò sobrio e tu sarai sempre brutta.

Spanish:
Yo puedo estar borracho, pero por
la manana yo estare sobrio y tu seguiras
siendo feo.

UGLY

**Please don't
smile until you've
seen a dentist.**

French:
S'il vous plaît, ne souriez pas avant
d'avoir vu un dentiste.

German:
Lächele bitte nicht bevor Du beim
Zahnarzt warst.

Italian:
Non sorridere se prima
non vai dal dentista.

Spanish:
Por favor, no sonrias hasta haber
visitado a un dentista.

UGLY

I think you're very brave to show your face in public without a paper bag to cover it.

French:
Je trouve que vous avez beaucoup de courage de vous montrer en public sans mettre un sac sur la tête.

German:
Du bist schon sehr mutig dich so in der Öffentlichkeit zeigen zu laßen ohne einen Sack auf dem Kopf zu tragen.

Italian:
Sei molto coraggioso di farti vedere in pubblico a volto scoperto.

Spanish:
Creo que eres muy valiente por mostrar tu cara en publico sin una bolsa que la cubra.

UGLY

Random Insults from Around the World

THE LITTLE BOOK OF

Afrikaans

fok jou:	fuck you
jy pis my af:	you're pissing me off
jou poes:	you cunt
moffie:	queer
poephol:	arsehole
jou doos:	you shithead
jou naai:	you fucking shit
jou simpel kont:	you stupid cunt
jy is vol kak:	you are full of shit
kontgesig:	cuntface

Arabic

boos teezee:	kiss my arse
charra alaik:	shit on you
cus:	fuck you
sharmute:	bastard
kul khara!:	eat shit!
shlicke:	slut
bouse tizi:	kiss my arse
reh tak khara:	you smell like shit
yakhreb beytak:	your arse smells bad
askut:	you're an eyesore

THE LITTLE BOOK OF

Brazilian Portuguese

chupe meu pau:	suck my nob
se fode:	fuck you
come merda:	eat shit
seu cara de cu:	you shitface
você é feio de doer:	you're an eyesore
vagabunda:	slut
mentecapto:	stupid twat
abilolado:	bloody idiot
paneleiro:	arse bandit
foda-se:	fuck off

Chinese (Cantonese)

fei hail:	fat cunt
gai:	whore
sek si:	eat shit
tiu nia ma chow hai:	fuck your mum's front bum
bat gong:	bastard

Chinese (Mandarin)

bil:	cunt
liu mang:	bastard
chao ni niang:	fuck your mother
ji nu:	whore
chuin-zi:	moron

Dutch

moederneuker:	motherfucker
schoft:	bastard
randdebiel:	stupid twat
gatlelijk:	ugly fucker
ga rukken:	toss off
rot op:	fuck off
rukker:	wanker
randdebiel:	divvy twat
oetlul:	idiot
eikel:	nobhead

Esperanto

anusulo:	arsehole
patrinfikulo:	motherfucker
ciesulino:	whore
forfikigi:	fuck off
fingrumo:	wanker

Greek

malakas:	wanker
ai gamisou:	fuck off
skata na fas:	eat poo
fae to louganigo mou:	suck my nob
mika ta kolo:	kiss my behind

Hebrew

lech zayen para:	Go fuck a cow
lakek et hatahat sheli:	Lick my arse
ben zsona:	son of a bitch
inahl Rabak Ars Ya Choosharmuta:	go to hell with your fucking father
stom ta'peh:	shut your cakehole

Japanese

baka:	stupid
bakayarou:	arsehole
chipatama:	dickhead
kusojiji:	old fart
kuso shite shinezo:	die shitting

Norwegian

morapuler:	motherfucker
fitte:	cunt
kuk suger:	nobsucker
stogging:	face like the back of a bus
fokk deg:	fuck you
jævla hore:	fucking prozzie
drittsek:	sack of shite
stikk a dra deg:	go and toss off
taper:	loser
baesj-puffer:	shit stabber

Russian

bl'ad:	bitch
govn'uk:	bastard
kurite moju trubku:	suck my cock
yeb vas:	fuck off
ëb tvoju mat':	fuck you

Serbian

govedo:	twat
jedi govno:	eat shit
picka:	cunt
kurvo razvaljena:	fucking bitch
podudlaj mi ga:	suck my dick

Swedish

knöllare:	fucker
sug min kuk:	suck my dick
skitpackare:	shit-packer
mutta:	cunt
tulle:	mud jouster

Welsh

cachau bant:	fuck off
wyneb cach:	shit face
cont tew:	fat cunt
bwyta fy gachu:	eat my excretion
pigyn bach:	tiny cock

EMMA BURGESS

THE LITTLE BOOK OF

ESSENTIAL FOREIGN SWEAR WORDS

summersdale *humour*

Ever been lost for words abroad? Impress the world with a stream of multi-lingual profanity from this nifty pocket book.

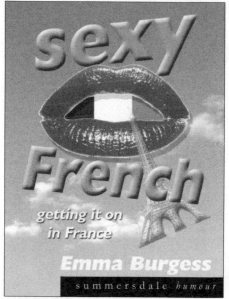

sexy/

French

*getting it on
in France*

Emma Burgess

summersdale *humour*

All the French phrases you'll need for flirting with a Frenchie, getting them into bed, and telling the doctor the next morning that it now hurts when you wee.

IRENE GRAHAM

SOD OFF!

THE
LITTLE
GUIDE TO
SOCIAL
AVOIDANCE

summersdale humour

This indispensable guide contains a myriad of suggestions to avoid unnecessary contact with the civilised world and ensure that the only person attending your birthday party is YOU.

www.summersdale.com